BATH
IN OLD PHOTOGRAPHS

BATH

IN OLD PHOTOGRAPHS

COLLECTED BY

JOHN HUDSON

ALAN SUTTON

Alan Sutton Publishing Limited
Phoenix Mill · Far Thrupp · Stroud · Gloucestershire

First published 1988

Reprinted 1993

British Library Cataloguing in Publication Data

Bath in old photographs.
1. Avon. Bath, history
I. Hudson, John
942.3'98

ISBN 0-86299-407-1

Typesetting and origination by
Alan Sutton Publishing Limited.
Printed in Great Britain by
WBC Limited, Bridgend.

CONTENTS

INTRODUCTION

I first saw Bath in 1962, shortly after poring over *Northanger Abbey* for English O-level. I did not know quite what to make of it then and, while the years in between have left me with far greater knowledge of the city, they have by no means ironed out all its contradictions.

Jane Austen's perception of the city was sharp and satirical, yet for all the fun she made of spa society the impression she left of the physical surroundings was one of almost unrelieved splendour. Perhaps it was simply that as a child growing up among the mill chimneys of the north of England, I had been conditioned to believe that all was well-heeled ease south of the Wash. Whatever the reason, as that train rolled me slowly past Stothert & Pitt's works in 1962, I felt like an actor sleeked up for a Noel Coward role who had found his script rewritten by John Osborne. I knew all about factories back home, but I had never seen anything remotely as nightmarish as Stothert & Pitt's . . .

It was the same when I arrived: unprepossessing Manvers Street, a jungle of new building and, when the walls of those streets and terraces of *Northanger Abbey* did at last open out before me, it was largely through a patina of grime. You only had to raise your eyes to roof level, and the batteries of chimney pots atop the elegant terraces, to see the reason; but it did not make the truth any more credible.

I feel that back in '62 there was still in the air an element of the Bath of this picture book, for better or worse. Most of this collection of photographs dates from the decade from 1900 to 1910, the heyday of the picture postcard, and the city's spirit of that time was much the same as it had been during Victoria's reign. It remained set in its ways through to the Second World War, the 1950s being a time of painful recovery, and it was not until the social and architectural revolution of the mid-1960s that Britain and Bath saw a future life very different from that of their forefathers.

Several generations of history wrapped up in a single paragraph? It is inadequate, I know, but to me there was a unifying factor in those times between Bath's Georgian spa glories and the high-profile city of the present – and that was a retreat to small-town provincialism. There were the architectural treasures, the Roman finds, the waters that would continue to attract increasingly more doddery and less fun-loving sufferers – but the city fathers had seen and heard enough of Beau Nash and the raffish and seedy years that both preceded and followed his reign, and they craved only the solid respectability that befitted the largest city in all of Somersetshire.

The spirit is reflected even in the picture postcards of the Edwardian years. For these and much else in the book I have drawn largely on the collections of Mr Peter Jones of Larkhall, Bath, and Mr Michael J. Tozer of Pill, Bristol, both of whom own several thousand images of the city. The photographers were moved scarcely at all by the Circus, the Royal Crescent, the Great Pulteney Street that had attracted kings and statesmen. They did as they would have done in Leicester or Reading and simply fired away in the High Street – or in Bath's case not the High Street at all, but the long, straight shopping thoroughfare that ran from the Old Bridge at the bottom of Southgate Street to the top of Union Street. For them, it seems that even Milsom Street was somewhat out on a limb; but if they could combine the shops with a hint of the history, as in the area around Stall Street fountain, then that was perfection.

Fortunately, there were times when staunch Victorian civic pride could make for a good picture. Bath was well enough aware of its history to know that it had to pull out the stops for jubilees, coronations and victory marches, and in doing so it left us with some indelible images. Nevertheless, the fact that Victoria never once visited the city as Queen is perhaps as telling an indication as any of the way in which the community, by and large, had been happy to sink back into the main pack, safe and anonymous.

That is not the way Bath does things today. An annual influx of millions of tourists and shoppers is vital to its economy, and the image the city presents is bright, cosmopolitan, and not so much solidly prosperous as rolling in wealth. You could almost say it is all I had dreamed it would be before my visit of 1962, though no-one at that time could quite have foreseen the chic slickness of today's consumer society. I stress that these observations are limited strictly to the image of the city now shown to the world at large. I need no reminding that today, as a century or two centuries ago, there is want and poverty in Bath, and that in between the extremes of those who inhabit the battered women's hostel and the Royal Crescent Hotel there are tens of thousands for whom the focal point of the city remains the trading centre of Stall Street and Southgate Street. People who shudder at the concrete and glass of that area today, and complain that it could belong to any middle-sized town in the country, will perhaps be cheered to look back on its anonymous forerunners of Edwardian times. Not exactly Wood the Elder masterpieces, are they?

Only on the city's inner fringes – the kind of streets down which tourists walk a few yards before consulting their maps and turning on their heels – will you see the smoke-blackened terraces so predominant before the big clean-up of the 1960s. Only Walcot Street of the areas most seen by visitors retains some of that down-at-heel air, mingled these days with the off-beat manifestations of Bath's alternative society. Again, there are pictures in this book to remind us that Walcot Street always *was* a bit odd, with its sheep markets surviving well into the age of the motor car.

And so they go on, the similarities, differences and *plus ça change* that make this collection of pictures, from so many helpful sources, quite fascinating to my eyes. If you are a native with memories of the city before the post-war changes I hope the book recalls happy times, and perhaps inspires you to give new thought to what was better about those days, and what worse. And if you are a visitor, the pictures will perhaps lead you to conclude that now is as happy a time to be in Bath as any since photography began. It is a view I would share – but if only there had been cameras a hundred years earlier to record the baths and the Beau and a lifestyle that made the city one of the playgrounds of Europe!

John Hudson, 1988

The Abbey and Pump Room

THE ABBEY CHURCHYARD in around 1906, with Bath chairs clustered around the entrance to the Pump Room and the Grand Pump Room Hotel in Stall Street looking imposing beyond the colonnade.

h, Bath Chairs and Pump Room.

BATH CHAIRS awaiting trade outside the Pump Room in around 1904. Some of the chairmen do not look exactly in their prime, but perhaps white whiskers sometimes adorned relatively young faces at the turn of the century. In the background is the fine west front of Bath Abbey, which has undergone considerable restoration since 1904. Very apparent on either side of the door are the church's famous sixteenth-century angels climbing (and in one case, falling off) ladders to heaven. They commemorate Bishop Oliver King, who inherited a sadly dilapidated Norman building on the site and set about restoring it after dreaming he saw a ladder to Paradise in 1499.

THE ABBEY CHURCHYARD in around 1890, with the left-hand side of the picture dominated by a building demolished in 1893 to make way for the Pump Room concert room. It comes as something of a shock, even in our capitalistic times, to see a site now so closely identified with the Abbey and Pump Room cheerfully plastered with advertisements for cricket and tennis gear, toys and beads. The picture on page 11 shows the new extension, then little more than ten years old.

A SCENE CONTEMPORARY with the one on the facing page; and below, the Abbey churchyard in the 1920s, updating the view seen on page 11.

Pump Room and Bath Abbey, Bath. 14686.

THE COOLING ROOM, above, a part of the spa complex fitted out, with no great lightness of touch, in around 1906. Below, the Pump Room fountain in the 1920s, in its alcove overlooking the King's Bath.

THE ATTENDANT SITS AT THE READY beside the mineral water fountain, and all is right with the world in this genteel Pump Room scene from around 1920.

THE GRAND PUMP ROOM, BATH, 10.

A PUMP ROOM SCENE dating from around 1912, although there is an air of timelessness about this particular corner of Bath. The building was started by the city architect Thomas Baldwin in 1789, but he was sacked in a financial dispute half-way through the project, and the interior is probably by his successor John Palmer. Among features that survive from an earlier Pump Room are a statue of Beau Nash, the master of ceremonies whose strict rules of conduct paved the way for Bath's predominance as an eighteenth-century spa resort, and a long-case clock presented by the celebrated London maker Thomas Tompion in 1709. Another statue is of Bladud, the mythical British prince said to have founded the city, while among the portraits is one of Ralph Allen, the benefactor who made one fortune out of a pioneering postal system and another from quarrying Bath stone at the height of the city's Georgian building boom.

THE EAST END OF BATH ABBEY: similar views from the Orange Grove, in 1890 and around 1930. The entrance canopy of the Empire Hotel, completed in 1901, can be seen beyond the car to the right of the lower photograph.

THE COLONNADE AND ABBEY, BATH.

FROM STALL STREET, a splendid view over the colonnade into the Abbey churchyard. This was the outlook enjoyed by guests with front rooms at the Grand Pump Room Hotel.

Heart of the City

THE LOWER END OF STALL STREET just before the First World War, with policemen finding no
great difficulty in controlling traffic flow at its junction with Lower Borough Walls and New
Orchard Street. Businesses include Newman's general store, Clark's furnishers, H. Sillett's
and Marsh's on the left, and Hallett's, Beasley & Crocker's haberdashery, the City Café,
Grant's and a branch of Lennards boot and shoe chain on the right.

BATH STREET in the 1930s, with Stall Street fountain and the Pump Room at the far end. The colonnaded Bath Street, linking the Roman Baths complex with the Cross Bath and designed in 1789, has been the subject of ambitious refurbishment plans in recent years.

TWO EARLY VIEWS of Stall Street fountain, the top one dating from around 1880, and the bottom from early this century, with a tram heading for Twerton. Archard's was a versatile shop, combining tailoring and jewellery with pawnbroking.

A CREEPER-CLAD FOUNTAIN dominates this view of Stall Street in around 1913. The Oldfield Park tram passes the Grand Pump Room Hotel and Royal Baths on the left and the Abbey churchyard colonnade on the right.

A SIMILAR SCENE to the one on page 23, some twenty years on in 1935. There is a clear view along Union Street to the corner of Upper Borough Walls, and the Combe Down tram lauds the contrasting delights of Mazawattee Tea and Symonds Ales. Another sign advertises Abdulla, one of the more exotic cigarette brands of the inter-war years.

A FAMILIAR NAME, though you will no longer find the American tourists' favourite store in Stall Street.

STALL STREET in the late nineteenth century, with the colonnade and Roman Baths complex on the left.

THE VIEW ALONG STALL STREET beyond the fountain reveals that the businesses south of the Bath Street junction almost uncannily reflect those of the neighbouring Archard's pictured on page 22. Comer & Watling's drapery warehouse stands alongside Arthur C. Quest's jewellery and pawnbroking business.

ANOTHER VIEW towards Union Street in the early 1900s.

A PLEASANT STALL STREET SCENE from 1906, capturing the charm of a city in which only the occasional passing tramcar gave a hint of traffic problems to come. With the Roman Baths and Pump Room, Royal Baths and Grand Pump Room Hotel all in this small corner, the Stall Street fountain was a major focal point for tourists in Victorian and Edwardian times.

THE IMPRESSIVE ENTRANCE to the Grand Pump Room Hotel in Stall Street in 1912. Built in the style of a large French seaside hotel, with pavilion roofs that would have looked very much at home in Deauville, the Grand Pump Room always offended Georgian purists and lasted less than ninety years, from 1870 to its demolition in 1959. The adjoining entrance to the New Royal Baths also disappeared then but the baths, opened in 1870 and latterly known as the Treatment Centre, continued until 1976. Their future as a private spa has been the subject of debate for several years.

CHEAP STREET'S JUNCTION with the High Street, with Cornish's butchery standing beside the entry to the Abbey churchyard. The Twerton tram advertises hosiery and gloves from Beasley & Crocker's round the corner in Stall Street, whose sign is visible in the picture on page 20.

WESTGATE STREET in the 1920s; to citizens of those times the Angel Hotel and Home & Colonial Stores seemed as much a part and parcel of Bath as the Abbey and Pump Room, yet now their names live on only in memory.

UNION STREET at its junction with Westgate and Cheap Streets. Like his counterparts at the bottom of Stall Street on page 20, the policeman seems unlikely to go home to tea suffering from nervous exhaustion.

THE CORRIDOR, between Union Passage and High Street, in around 1905. Built in 1825, this elegant covered walkway boasts a musicians' gallery, scarcely a priority of shopping malls of the late twentieth century. It is interesting to note that hanging baskets were *de rigueur* here decades before the annual Britain in Bloom contest.

THE GUILDHALL seen from outside Cornish's butcher's shop in 1906. This impressive complex, with a small number of sumptuous and exquisitely decorated state rooms open to the public, was built in the years around 1770 by Thomas Baldwin, a city architect who made a greater mark on the Georgian city than many a more exalted name. On the right of the picture is the Victorian fountain of Rebecca at the well, with its resounding temperance message 'Water Is Best'.

FOUR BATH ELECTRIC TRAMWAYS BUSES at the Guildhall, loading for an outing to the country. The one in the front came in a batch of six bought by the company in 1906.

THE HIGH STREET in 1906, with the Christopher Hotel and Guildhall prominent.

GUINEA PIG JACK.

GUINEA PIG JACK was one of Bath's best-known street entertainers at the turn of the century, a perhaps timely reminder that the buskers who cluster around Stall Street and Union Street today, to the occasional displeasure of the law, are part of a long tradition. History does not record exactly how Jack's charges performed. Perhaps he picked them up by the tail and their eyes fell out, the stunt most usually accredited to this particular creature.

The Bath Historical Pageant, 1909

ATH DECORATED — HIGH ST & GUILDHALL.
19TH JULY 1909. N93.

THE BATH HISTORICAL PAGEANT was the high spot of the summer of 1909, though from the previous autumn well over two thousand citizens were learning their lines and sewing their costumes in preparation for it. It told the history of Bath from Roman to Regency times, but amateur dramatics were only a part of it. The town dressed itself up like never before, an effort that seems all the more amazing when one considers that in little more than twenty years it had celebrated two royal jubilees, a coronation and the homecoming of the boys from South Africa. Perhaps if the organisers had had a premonition of the imminent death of Edward VII, and yet another coronation, they might have thought again. This is the scene in the High Street outside the Guildhall; more on the 'Bath Pageant 1909' tram on page 42.

THE SCENE in Union Street.

NEW BOND STREET'S EFFORTS in the pageant celebrations, with the traders on the left-hand side making by far the braver show.

DECORATIONS SO GRAND you can only stand and stare . . . Cheap Street greets the pageant in style.

EALAND'S OUTFITTERS on the corner of New Bond Street, a site now occupied by Habitat.

THE PAGEANT TRAM pictured with *Bristol Echo* newsboys, for reasons known only to some long-gone circulation manager. The tram acted as a booking office, as well as advertising the tramway company's tours and excursions.

THE DUKE OF CONNAUGHT arrives to open the pageant.

The Bath Historical Pageant, 1909.

Miss English as "Rusonia Avenna in Dedication of Sul's Temple. Lewis Bros, Official Photographers.

A FORMIDABLE MISS ENGLISH as the Roman Rusonia Avenna at the temple of Sulis Minerva.

The Bath Historical Pageant, 1909. King Bladud & the Pigs   Lewis Bros. Official Photographers

BLADUD AND HIS PIGS in Royal Victoria Park. The legend of the prince is that he was exiled as a swineherd when he contracted leprosy, only to return to his father's court in triumph after his pigs had led him into Bath's health-giving spring. Perhaps he should have settled for just the one miracle: according to his myth, he died while trying to fly with home-made wings.

SAXON WARRIORS – one of a number of bands. Groups of workmates teamed up to do their bit for the pageant.

MERRIE ENGLAND: the Elizabethan Maypole scene was one of the most popular of the pageant.

THE GLORIOUS TIMES OF BEAU NASH: scarcely surprisingly, the pageant leaned heavily on Georgian lore and tradition in the build-up to its grand finale.

STARS AND STRIPES and Statue of Liberty head-dresses brought the Bath Historical Pageant to its end, with Lady de Blaquiere, centre, as Ladye Bath. Her attendants are all from different towns named Bath in the United States and Canada, a small indication of the organisational effort that went into the venture at a time when a trip across the Atlantic involved rather more than an afternoon of watching in-flight movies.

THE PAGEANT'S MASTER OF CEREMONIES was Frank Lascelles, who is seen receiving a commemorative gift from Lady de Blaquiere.

Milsom Street and the Upper City

LOOKING EASTWARD along Quiet Street to the lower end of Milsom Street, with L.E. Penwarden and Walker & Ling's shops prominent on the left.

A DISPLAY of Henry Heath Hats at Walker & Ling's in Milsom Street. The store traded as 'The House of a Thousand Novelties', and it need hardly be said that this display of cloche styles dates from the twenties – November 1928, to be exact. In Jane Austen's *Northanger Abbey* of 1818 it was in Milsom Street that Isabella Thorpe spotted 'the prettiest little hat you can imagine in a shop window'.

COBBLESTONES: shoppers walking peacefully in the carriageway ... Milsom Street in 1910.

THE BATH BANK at the corner of the lower end of Milsom Street and Green Street, a remarkable early photograph of around 1870.

HOLIDAY CROWDS in Milsom Street in the early years of this century.

BATH. — Milsom Street. — LL.

ANOTHER LIVELY SCENE in Milsom Street in around 1906. There is a total absence of motorised traffic, yet the bustle and vitality of the city's most prestigious shopping street is unmistakable.

A. VEZEY'S BUTCHER'S SHOP at 10 Green Street advertises 'All English Beef This Week', but it scarcely looks appetising to today's tastes. Leaving aside questions of hygiene, those joints hanging round the door look a hundred times more like dead animals chopped up than the supermarket offerings of our times.

Milsom Street Bath

MILSOM STREET has almost a film-set quality in this view, presumably taken with a telescopic lens from an upper window in Edgar Buildings, George Street. The total traffic on the street consists of a handcart and three horse-drawn vehicles, one of which is at right-angles to the carriageway in the act of turning.

LAWRENCE'S FRUIT VAN around the time of the First World War. The family had a shop at the bottom of Milsom Street in Burton Street.

MILSOM STREET dressed overall for the Diamond Jubilee of 1897, with festoons of flowers and evergreens combined with coloured lights and gas illuminations on the footpaths. One wonders how long the photographer in Edgar Buildings waited for the horse-drawn trap; whether by accident or design, it turns the picture from a fascinating historical record into something approaching art.

THE THEATRE ROYAL in Sawclose in around 1908, the current show being Wilson Barrett's *Lucky Durham*. The theatre was built in 1805 to replace an earlier one in Orchard Street – see the opening playbill on page 88 – but its front was on Beaufort Square until a fire in 1862 brought major changes. This Italianate porch dates from that time and it offends classical purists, while seeming attractive enough to the layman. There was even some talk of demolishing it when the theatre was refurbished in the early 1980s.

THE THEATRE ROYAL'S NEAR NEIGHBOUR in Upper Borough Walls, the Blue Coat Charity School of 1860. With its Jacobean gables it is yet another building that causes grief to the neo-Georgians.

IF YOU WANTED TO HIRE A HORSE in Victorian and Edwardian Bath you made your way to the Ames stables in Barton Street.

LOOKING ALONG THE EAST SIDE of Queen Square to Barton Street and Sawclose in the 1930s, with King Street to the left. Queen Square was developed to resemble a palace courtyard with the imposing terrace to the north the focal point, but this eastern flank retains a pleasingly domestic scale.

LOOKING NORTH TOWARDS GAY STREET along the eastern side of Queen Square, with a fine array of cars on view. The absence of foliage reveals the terrace to the north of the square. Some lovers of Bath feel that trees detract from the likes of Queen Square and The Circus, though one can imagine the outcry should any serious moves ever be made to clear them.

THE FRANCIS HOTEL at the southern end of Queen Square in the 1930s, looking along Wood and Quiet streets towards Milsom Street, with the spire of St Michael's, Broad Street, beyond. A picture of the hotel some ten years on, and in less happy times, appears on page 157.

THE WAR MEMORIAL beside the lion gateposts at the bottom of Royal Avenue was unveiled for Armistice Day 1927 and is seen here a few years later. One reason for the delay was the formidable task of drawing up a comprehensive list of the city's casualties.

'FROM TROUBLES OF THE WORLD I turn to ducks . . .' (F.W. Harvey). A gentle scene in Royal Victoria Park.

TWO VIEWS OF THE ASSEMBLY ROOMS in Bennett Street in the 1920s, when they were suffering the indignity of being used as a cinema. They were built by Wood the Younger in three years around 1770, but it was not always easy to find a use for them after their spa heyday. Ironically, the severe damage they suffered during the Second World War can perhaps now be seen as a blessing in heavy disguise. They were restored with great care and attention to detail in the 1960s; their magnificent state rooms are now in the hands of the National Trust, and in the basement the imaginatively-presented Museum of Costume houses a collection of international importance.

MARGARET'S BUILDINGS, off Brock Street, in 1904. Present-day businesses in this civilised little backwater off the main route to Royal Crescent deal in such exotica as South American statues and Venetian carnival masks, but there remain a few shops catering for everyday needs. A baker's boy from the Royal Crescent Bakery poses beside the Bath chair.

ST JAMES'S SQUARE in around 1914, with the silhouette of an army officer among those captured by the strong evening light.

SECTION FIVE

The First World War

COMBE PARK was the site of Bath's temporary 1,000-bed war hospital from the First World War until 1929. Above we see the entrance, manned by able-bodied soldiers, and below, a group of patients outside three of the wards.

Dispensary. Bath War Hospital.
1426.

TWO IMPORTANT FOCAL POINTS of the war hospital, the dispensary and kitchen.

The Kitchen, Bath War Hospital.
1902.

New Marque Section,
Bath War Hospital. 16/2

AS CASUALTIES IN EUROPE hit a peak in 1916 and 1917 the war hospital was forced to house some of its less seriously injured patients in a tented village.

New Marquee Section, Bath War Hospital. 1649.

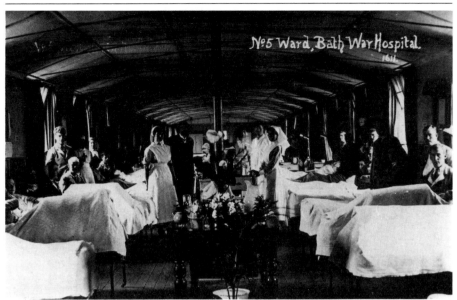

A TYPICAL SCENE in one of the overcrowded wards and, below, billiards and wicker chairs in the YMCA hut.

THE ROYAL MINERAL HOSPITAL was also commandeered for war casualties, well over 3,000 being treated there. This is the scene in the electrical treatment room, where overcrowding again appears to be severe.

SOLDIERS OUTSIDE THEIR BILLETS in Park Street, leading up to Lansdown, in 1917. The message on the back of the postcard, from Private Will Harris to his father in Stafford, reads: 'Dear Dad, This is where I am billetted. I was on guard at the top of this street on Saturday. It is very steep.'

ABLE-BODIED TROOPS camping at Lansdown, those in the lower picture allowing themselves the luxury of civvies.

INVALIDED TROOPS and their nurses on a visit to the Roman Baths in July 1916. The ill-fitting blue suits of disabled soldiers usually gave them a pathetic and institutional air, but this group seems almost languidly elegant, like a hunting party at some exotic spot. It must have been marvellous to leave the confines of the camp.

The Lower City

CHRISTMAS DISPLAY at William Mead's greengrocer's, 12 Claverton Buildings.

DORCHESTER STREET in the 1930s, with Stanley Marks & Werry's confectioner's van prominent.

LOOKING SOUTH ACROSS THE OLD BRIDGE from Southgate Street in around 1908; the bridge was replaced by the Churchill Bridge, slightly to the west, in 1966. The Oldfield Park tram seen here was brought into service in August 1905 and survived until the eve of the Second World War.

LOOKING NORTH ALONG SOUTHGATE STREET from the Old Bridge in around 1906. It is high summer, and the hoardings beside the river advertise an athletics festival and a fête in Sydney Gardens. The Full Moon was a noted coaching inn in Bath's Georgian heyday, but this building dated only from the 1830s. It was demolished between the wars to make way for an electricity showroom.

GEORGE MILLER'S tobacconist's shop in Southgate Street, 1906.

MEN AT WORK at 11 Southgate Street, around 1905 to 1910. The results of their efforts can be seen overleaf.

GOULSTONE'S VICTORIA TEMPERANCE HOTEL, 11 and 12 Southgate Street, shortly before the First World War. Hot dinners from 6d. must have been an inviting prospect for many a weary 'commercial' and cyclist.

SOUTHGATE STREET in around 1907. Businesses include Holloway's butchers, Hodders the chemists, Glendells and Furze's Dining Room on the left, and on the right, F. Budgett, Pratley and Blatchford.

THE LONG-ESTABLISHED Evans's Fish Bar still flourishes. This photograph shows its Abbeygate Street premises in 1919.

ROBERT WHITE'S potato trucks behind his shop in James Street West in around 1920.

THESE HOUSES IN AVON STREET have long since gone, but older Bath residents still remember this and the neighbouring Milk Street as a rough, tough area in which poverty was rife. The woman to the right of the group wears a heavy industrial apron, suggesting that she was employed in hard physical work.

MILK STREET RESIDENTS: Emma Whittington and her son Fred.

ABBEY CHURCH HOUSE in the 1930s. Although rebuilt after war damage, this fine Elizabethan building off Lower Borough Walls continues to hint at the atmosphere of old Bath before the Georgian developers moved in.

ABBEY CHURCH HOUSE in 1885. At this time it was known as Hetling House after an eighteenth-century owner, receiving its current name when the rector and churchwardens of Bath Abbey acquired it in 1888. The cluster of street urchins around the door suggest that it was used for some charitable purpose.

CHARLES STREET in around 1910 – early November, judging by the advertisements for fireworks in the newsagent's shop beside the Green Park Dairy. Another sign publicises Rajah cigars, at a modest 2*d*. each or seven for a shilling (5p).

KINGSMEAD SQUARE in about 1906; the Weston tram dates from two years before then. Rosewell House, opened in 1736, is the most ornate building in the city, a late flourishing of Baroque in a community where clean, classical lines were already becoming the *sine qua non*. 'Nothing save ornaments without taste', was the Younger Wood's judgment.

A FAMILIAR SIGHT around the city streets: a Bath & Somersetshire Dairy milk boy, this one immaculately kitted out and obviously destined to own a horse-drawn float or two before his days were through.

Bath at Play

DIDN'T THEY PACK THEM IN? A Bath Electric Tramways AEC charabanc with a party bound for Wilton House.

REMEMBER THE SCENE in *A Midsummer Night's Dream*? These are the girls who brought it to life in an Oldfield Council Senior Girls' School performance in the 1920s.

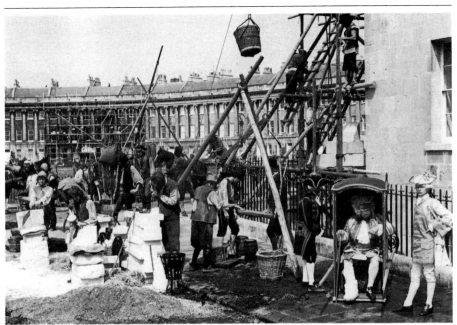

ABOVE, A RARE PHOTOGRAPH of the building of the Royal Crescent in around 1770 – or at least, the stage set-designer's version of it in the location filming of *Joseph Andrews* in 1977. Below, a scene at the Abbey churchyard colonnade during the making of another film, *Lord Vanity*, a generation earlier. All the cameras and lights caused a great stir at the time, but nobody seems to remember much about the end result today.

THE WELL-TURNED-OUT Bath Military Band with their conductor, Mr W.F.C. Schottler, in 1905. Below, things seem a little more relaxed at this band concert in Royal Victoria Park in the 1920s.

THE MERRYMAKERS CONCERT PARTY at Sydney Gardens in 1908. The message on the back of the postcard gives the impression they were not quite London Palladium material.

NEW THEATRE - ROYAL.

Beaufort-Square, Bath,

Will OPEN on SATURDAY next, OCT. 12. 1805,

With Shakespeare's Hiftorical TRAGEDY of

King Richard III.

With entire new Scenery, Machinery, and other Decorations.

Richard, Duke of Glofter - By A YOUNG GENTLEMAN,
(His Firft Appearance on any Stage.)
King Henry the Sixth - - Mr. CHARLTON.
Prince of Wales Mifs MARTIN. | Duke of York Mifs L. QUICK.
Duke of Buckingham - - Mr. CAULFIELD,
(From the Theatre-Royal, Drury-Lane, his Firft Appearance on the Bath Stage)
Duke of Norfolk Mr. EGAN. | Earl of Oxford Mr. ABBOTT.
Henry, Earl of Richmond - Mr. EGERTON.
Lord Stanley - - - - Mr. RICHARDSON,
(His Firft Appearance here thefe three years.)
Lord Mayor of London - Mr. EVANS.
Sir W. Brandon - - - Mr. CUNNINGHAM.
Sir Richard Ratcliffe - - Mr. CUSHING,
(His Firft Appearance here.)
Sir William Catefby - - Mr. GOMERY.
Sir Robert Brackenbury - - Mr. GATTIE.
Sir James Tyrrel - - - Mr. KELLY.
Sir James Blunt - - - Mr. EDWARDS.
Dighton - - - - - Mr. LODGE.
Foreft - - - - - Mr. SIMS.

Queen Elizabeth - - - Mifs FISHER.
Duchefs of York Mrs. CHARLTON. | Lady Anne - Mifs JAMESON.

To which will be added the Mufical FARCE of THE

POOR SOLDIER.

Patrick - - - - - - - Mifs WHEATLY,
(From the Theatre-Royal, Covent-Garden, her firft appearance on this Stage.)
Father Luke - - - Mr. RICHARDSON. | Capt. Fitzroy - - - Mr. CUSHING.
Dermot - - - - Mr. WEBBER. | Bagatelle - - - - Mr. GATTIE.
Darby - - - - - - Mr. MALLINSON.
Kathleen - - - - - - - - - Mrs. SIMS.
Norah - - - - - - - - - - Mrs. WINDSOR.

Boxes 5s.---Pit 3s.---Gallery 1s. 6d. Latter Account, Boxes 3s.---Pit 2s.---Gallery 1s.
Tickets and Places for the Boxes to be taken of Mr. BARTLEY, at his Houfe in Orange-court, Grove.

ANN KEENE, PRINTER, KINGSMEAD STREET, BATH.

THE PLAYBILL for the first production at the present Theatre Royal, which then had its main entrance in Beaufort Square. As was quite common in those times, the Shakespeare history play was leavened with a 'musical farce', with several actors appearing in both.

AMATEUR ACTORS recreating a scene from Beau Nash's time in the Pump Room for the Bath Assembly of 1948. From small beginnings after the last war the assembly went on to develop into Bath's world-famous summer music festival.

SCHOOL PLAYTIME — if only the photographer would go away and let them get on with it — at the Convent of the Holy Union of Sacred Hearts in 1907, above, and at Hamilton House, Lansdown, at much the same time.

A BATH CHARA OUTING picnicking in the country. They are supporting home industries with a flagon of Bowler's ginger pop.

THE TINKLE OF SILVER on china at the Glasshouse Café Tea Gardens in 1925.

THE EARLY AUTUMN BATH HORSE SHOW in late Edwardian times. The picture above was used by Jolly's, then as now of Milsom Street, to promote their warm outdoor clothing.

BATH HORSE SHOW,
1st & 2nd Sept., 1909.

"OLD ENGLISH FAIR" BATH CARNIVAL WEEK 1911

BATH CARNIVAL TIME: the motley crew above dates from 1911, probably very much the same time as the Rotarians were drumming up support in their usual way with the help of the tramway company.

Rotary Club. Rotary Club

GIVE YOUR SUPPORT TO THOSE IN NEED EVERY COPPER HELPS.

THE CLEAN-CUT YOUNG MEN of Walcot rugby club in 1905–6 – and below, a rather more dubious bunch of lads with an even more dubious bunch of dogs.

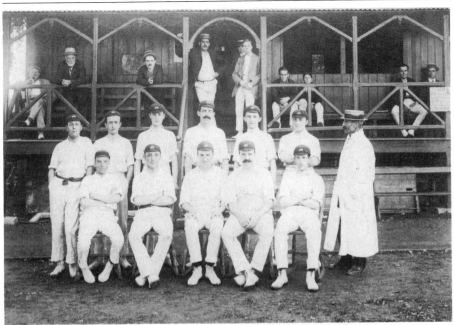

TWO VINTAGE BATH POST OFFICE CRICKET TEAMS, the lower one from 1904.

BATH FIRST AVIATION MEETING GRAHAME WHITE ON HIS AEROPLANE, MAY 1912

THE YEAR FLYING CAUGHT THE IMAGINATION OF THE PUBLIC WAS 1912, with the first *Daily Mail* Round-Britain Race. Bath had its inaugural air show in that year, too, when the ace Grahame White was the big heart-throb with his biplane and natty attire.

Bathwick Boating Station, Bath.

BOATING WITH THE GIRLS on the Avon at Bathwick, 1920s.

IT ALL LOOKS A BIT SPARTAN for the little boys at Clevedon Baths at Bathwick in 1907; the scene below at the main pool of the Royal Baths is much more cosy, mixed bathing and all.

Mixed Bathing, Bath

A PANORAMIC VIEW of the Royal Baths' main pool in around 1906.

LOCAL SOCCER TEAMS of Edwardian days, the Manvers Street Institute second eleven of 1909–10, above, looking particularly purposeful.

CAMILLA 'POPPY' DAVIS was a Bath beauty queen in around 1911, and it is not hard to see why.

DORIEN CUFF, Bath Rotary Carnival Queen in 1934. A local girl of the same surname won a major national beauty contest a few years ago. Does it run in the family?

The East City Centre

32   BATH. — Museum and Library. — LL.

THE ABOVE PICTURE and the one on the facing page of Pierrepont Street and Terrace Walk are taken from an almost identical angle. This was the site of the Lower Assembly Rooms of Jane Austen's *Northanger Abbey*. When they were demolished in 1823 the Royal Literary and Scientific Institution was built rather broodingly in their place. It housed a geological and Roman museum until 1933, when it made way for road improvements. The horse-drawn bus seen outside it in this picture from 1906 picked up hotel guests from the railway stations.

THE FERNLEY HOTEL in North Parade and, below, the scene looking south from the Empire Hotel, with the Parade Gardens in the foreground.

General View from Empire Hotel, Bath.   2670. 1

THE ORNATE little ornamental lodges of North Parade Bridge.

JOHN WOOD THE ELDER'S South Parade in Edwardian times; a handful of decorative early pillar boxes still survive in Bath.

STATELY PIERREPONT STREET, with the clean lines of Wood the Elder's terraces of the 1740s spoiled, in some purists' eyes, by the Victorians' florid Empire Hotel peeping over their shoulders.

MANVERS STREET in around 1906, with a fine array of advertising hoardings on the left.

PREPARED: Manvers Street Institute Boy Scouts and their mentors.

BATH. - *Empire Hotel from Orange Grove* — LL.

HIRE CARRIAGES and an early motor wagonette line up in the Orange Grove outside the Empire Hotel in around 1906. The splendidly situated hotel, built in 1901, was requisitioned by the Admiralty during the Second World War, and only in the late 1980s has there been serious discussion about the possibility of its returning to its original use. For all that the architectural critic Pevsner says about its 'unbelievable' style, one cannot imagine that tourists with unrivalled views of the Abbey or Pulteney Bridge would have many qualms.

ONLY A HANDFUL OF YEARS after the picture opposite, perhaps 1910 – yet the waiting cabs speak of another age of travel. These were Bristol Tramways Blue Taxis, set up in rivalry to the local firms.

BUS QUEUES in Grand Parade in the summer of 1933.

Empire Hotel, Bath.

THE EMPIRE HOTEL from the Parade Gardens, known as the Institutional Gardens until the demolition of the Royal Literary and Scientific Institution in 1933 (see page 102).

THE EMPIRE HOTEL'S courtesy bus.

THE SOUTH FAÇADE of Robert Adam's 1770 masterpiece, Pulteney Bridge, in 1905, still blighted by the odd outbuilding tagged on to expand cramped and narrow shop spaces. The concerted effort to tidy up the view of the bridge from Grand Parade was one of Bath's greatest conservation triumphs.

A VIEW OF THE BRIDGE of much the same date, with Edwardian ladies taking the air on the Grand Parade.

THE WEST END of Pulteney Bridge, with the musical shop Duck Son & Pinker's dominating the northern shopping parade, as it does to this day.

ARTHUR GODDARD'S fruit and vegetable shop on the corner of Pulteney Bridge and Grand Parade – a reminder of how much the bridge was regarded as a working street, rather than a tourist attraction. Indeed, it remains the case to this day that most of the shopping space on the bridge serves local needs, rather than the demands of souvenir-hunters.

LAURA PLACE in around 1912, looking down Argyle Street to Pulteney Bridge. The fountain was put up in 1877 to mark the centenary of the Bath and West Society.

LAURA PLACE and Great Pulteney Street in around 1907, with the Bath hoteliers' bus outside the Pulteney Hotel on the left. The hotel was one of the most splendid in the city, attracting a string of titled guests.

SYDNEY GARDENS at the end of Great Pulteney Street were a social focal point of Georgian Bath, but by the time this picture was taken, in around 1913, their glory days were long gone. The little classical shelter was built in 1909 to mark the Bath Pageant, its front being a replica of the temple of Sulis Minerva still being excavated beneath the Pump Room. It survives, although like its great original it has seen better days.

THE SHEEP MARKET in Walcot Street in around 1906. To the right of the lower picture is the Catherine Wheel pub, with beside it a sign advertising 'Well Aired Beds'.

WALCOT STREET in the 1920s; on the right, beside the splendid Peak, Frean's biscuit van, is Horton Brothers' auctioneers and furnishers business.

CLEVELAND TERRACE, London Road in around 1910, with the turning into Cleveland Place and the bridge. Cleveland Place, built some five years later than the bridge in 1832, was designed by the same architect, Henry Edmund Goodridge.

THE HUMANE SOCIETY station in one of Cleveland Bridge's sturdy Greek Doric toll houses in around 1907.

THE RIVERS ARMS PUB in Camden Road in around 1910, singing the praises of Bath Brewery's Oatmeal Stout. The building remains, though much altered.

SECTION NINE

Transport

WORKERS LINE UP for a team photograph on a giant hammerhead crane at Stothert & Pitt's yard in the early years of this century. The cranemakers are perhaps the city's most famous industry, carrying the name of Bath around the world. When the first photographs of the submerged *Titanic* were released in the early 1980s, among the first items identified was a Stothert & Pitt deck-mounted crane.

A LOCO IN THE RAIL YARD beside Stothert & Pitt's plant during the First World War. Several of the workers are women, and with the odd exception the average age would seem to be around 16.

THE SCENE OUTSIDE THE GREAT WESTERN RAILWAY STATION, Bath Spa, in around 1906. A metal footbridge links the station hotel, now the Berni Royal, with the station at platform level.

BATH 1932

IN THE DAYS WHEN A MAN'S LABOUR WAS CHEAP: a track gang at the GWR station in 1932.

BATH ELECTRIC TRAMWAYS TRAM runs out of control from Combe Park to the bottom of Locksbrook Hill, April 1904.

ANOTHER BATH ELECTRIC TRAMWAYS TRAM runs out of control from Newbridge Road to the junction at the Weston Hotel in Lower Weston, 29 May 1918. A local councillor is killed – and what is worse for suffragettes and feminists, the driver is a woman. In spite of the shortage of men during the war, the company barred female workers from driving its vehicles for several years after this.

THE OLD MIDLAND BRIDGE

WORK ON THE OLD MIDLAND BRIDGE seems to be attracting a great deal of interest, though its significance is lost on most local historians. The fact that a policeman seems to be keeping guard over the scene suggests that it is something other than routine maintenance.

THE ELEGANT TRAIN SHED of the Midland Railway station, pictured around 1880, which became Green Park station after nationalisation, and is today a feature of one of the world's most impressive supermarket car-parks.

*8o BATH. — Midland
Railway Station. — LI*

A BUSY SCENE ON THE MIDLAND RAILWAY STATION at Green Park. The station was opened in 1870, its classical façade blending far more admirably with the spirit of Bath than Brunel's earlier GWR Tudor at the end of Manvers Street. A product of the intense early rivalry between the railway companies, the Midland station was a terminus into which trains between Bournemouth and the North and Midlands detoured courtesy of Somerset and Dorset Joint Railway tracks.

THOSE WHO REMEMBER BRITISH RAILWAY TERMINI during the age of steam will be astonished by this photograph of Bath's Midland station in 1938. There is an almost Continental air of space, light, calm and cleanliness, and the station-master and his staff, seen to the right, deserve a more prominent place in the picture. There is nothing Continental about the advertising hoardings, however: good old Brylcreem, plus some samples of those classic inter-war railway posters that make such attractive postcards today.

ON BORROWED TIME: neither Green Park station nor the steam loco had very long to go when this beautifully atmospheric photograph was taken in 1962.

SECTION TEN

On the Fringes

THE TEMPERANCE HALL of 1847 in Claverton Street, pictured in the early 1930s. The film advertised at the Assembly Rooms is a curio: *Monsieur Beaucaire*, a Rudolph Valentino vehicle apparently set in eighteenth-century Bath. A pity for Rudy's myriad fans that it was not filmed on location.

A BRISTOL-BUILT BATH ELECTRIC TRAMWAYS BUS of 1906 pictured outside the Belvoir Castle pub in Lower Bristol Road shortly after that date. There was room for 18 on top, 17 inside, and the passengers here seem intent on proving the point.

A VIEW OF BEECHEN CLIFF – rather than the far more usual view *from* Beechen Cliff – in around 1930.

THE SHAM CASTLE overlooking the city from the east was scarcely a folly. Ralph Allen had it put there in the eighteenth century to improve the view from his town house in York Street and besides, it served as an excellent advertisement for his Bath stone.

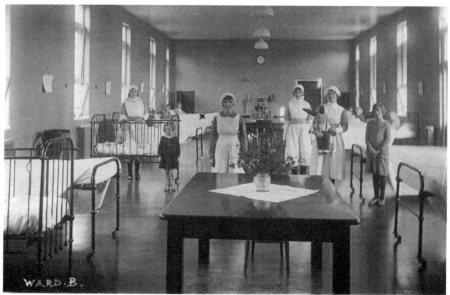

CLEAN, FUNCTIONAL, BRIGHT, AIRY — and somewhere you would rather not be. The Statutory Hospital at Claverton Down, stemming from an isolation hospital founded in the 1830s.

A CREEPER-CLAD ST MARY'S CHURCH, Charlcombe, a couple of generations after its Victorian restoration of 1861. The church is of ancient foundation, with Norman doorways and font.

STRIDE'S FREE HOUSE PUB AND BREWERY at Odd Down at around the time of the First World War.

THE LARKHALL INN, still instantly recognisable today, in the steep and sometimes maze-like upland suburbs to the north-east of the city. A child with a hoop outside the pub door is among the passers-by who stood in suspended animation while the photographer recorded the scene.

ANOTHER VIEW OF LARKHALL, this one of the cluster of shops in St Saviour's Road. Hoops were obviously quite the thing in these steep and quiet streets, and a child stands with one between Gray's Victoria Bakery and John Garraway's shop.

WESTON. The pictures on these two pages are of the north-western suburb of Weston, showing (above) the tramway terminus, school and All Saints' Church tower; (below) the steep Church Road, where the milkman delivering with churns on a yoke must have found the going tough; (top right) the Park Tavern and Park Lane; and (lower right) washday in the High Street. These pictures serve as an appetiser for a full book of views from the Bath fringes to be produced by Alan Sutton Publishing at a later date.

WIDCOMBE, BATH

ANOTHER SUBURBAN HIGH STREET in its own right: workaday Widcombe in 1904.

THE NORTH-EASTERN SUBURB OF KENSINGTON on a snowy, slushy day in around 1910, in which the tramway certainly appears to be the most reliable form of transport. One of the posters on the left advertises the actor-manager F.R. Benson's Shakespearian company at the Theatre Royal.

A FAMILY GROUP pictured in the 1920s by H. Long of Entry Hill, a prolific local photographer of the day. A low-key wedding, perhaps, or an anniversary for the couple in the centre? The exact nature of the event is not clear, but everyone seems cheerful enough about it.

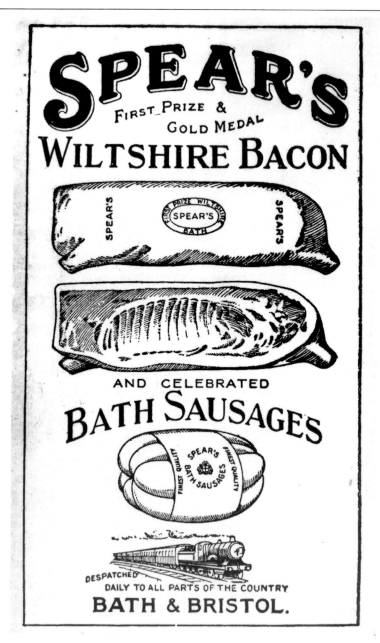

SPEAR'S

FIRST PRIZE &
GOLD MEDAL

WILTSHIRE BACON

AND CELEBRATED

BATH SAUSAGES

DESPATCHED
DAILY TO ALL PARTS OF THE COUNTRY

BATH & BRISTOL.

A HOME INDUSTRY that tens of thousands of Bathonians were more than happy to support at least once a week; there are still folk in the city who go misty-eyed when they speak of Spear's sausages.

High Days, Low Days

FLOODS were a fact of life in the streets to the south of the city centre until well into this century, bringing extra misery to citizens already living in wretched conditions. That having been said, there is something almost artistic about this study of St James Street, with a man on a makeshift raft leaving an unforgettable image as he paddles between Trinity Church and the Midland Hotel on 25 October 1882.

ANOTHER MEMORABLE VIEW OF ST JAMES STREET in 1882; it must have been an exciting sight if all your worldly goods did not happen to be under six feet of water at the time.

THE FLOODS IN SOUTHGATE STREET in 1895; as always, it did not take good neighbours long to rise to the occasion and check on everyone's safety by boat.

ON TO THE 1920s – and Southgate Street is deep in it again. The film showing at the Picturedrome is Hoot Gibson's western *The Thrill Chaser*, but you feel that this is one occasion when even the US Cavalry would have been hard pressed to save the day.

BACK ON DRY LAND AT LAST, on Cleveland Bridge on 22 June 1919. The Mayor is shaking hands with the Marquess of Bath, the Lord Lieutenant of Somerset, who has just freed this and other city bridges of tolls.

VICTORIA'S GOLDEN JUBILEE of 1887 was celebrated cheerfully all over the country. The Queen had kept a low profile after Albert's death, and there were times during the middle of her reign when she could scarcely be said to have been popular, simply because she so rarely impinged on her nation's consciousness. It remains a fact, for instance, that she never once visited Bath as a monarch, an astonishing record in an age of railway travel. But by the time the Golden Jubilee came around the city was happy to join the rest of the nation in saluting her, and ten years later the Diamond Jubilee was even more heartily celebrated. This bust of the Queen from the earlier celebrations is thought to have been in Milsom Street.

THE DIAMOND JUBILEE in 1897, and three bullocks are roasted for 'deserving recipients' in Royal Victoria Park.

BROAD STREET *en fête* for the 1897 Jubilee. Would Her Majesty have been amused by the cricket fan's salute?

HOLIDAY CROWDS celebrate the 1897 Jubilee in Laura Place.

A SUNNY DAY and a fine turn-out as the Mayor lays the foundation stone for J.M. Brydon's Guildhall extensions on 1 June 1893. The wing now houses the city's art gallery and lending library.

THE CITY'S OWN REGIMENT, the Bath Volunteers, were a great draw whenever they marched in force through the streets. The picture above shows them wheeling into High Street after returning from the Boer War in 1902. Below, the crowds in Queen Square, possibly on the same occasion.

84   BATH. — Volunteers in Queen's Garden. — LL.

CHURCH PROCESSION THROUGH THE ABBEY CHURCHYARD, with a variety of uniformed organi-
sations, including the Boy Scouts. Presumably around the time of the First World War, the
exact nature of the event is unknown.

CROWDS STAND UP TO TEN DEEP to watch a funeral procession at St Andrew's Church, Julian Road in around 1910.

AN EARLY GIRL GUIDE RALLY in the Abbey churchyard; the movement was founded in 1910, and the inspection on this occasion was by a member of the Baden Powell family.

BRISTOL TRAMWAYS & CARRIAGE CO. opened its Blue Taxi branch in James Street West in 1909, competing with earlier city-based companies. Edward VII died in the following year, and it could be that this patriotic display marked George V's coronation.

THE SUNDAY SCHOOL BANNER, Ebenezer Baptist Tabernacle.

HITLER'S AERIAL OFFENSIVES against historic British cities were known as the Baedeker raids, after the German tourists' guidebooks. The blackspot for Bath was 25–26 April 1942, when more than 400 people were killed and 200 historic buildings destroyed. Above, the morning after at the Francis Hotel, Queen Square; and below, Lansdown Place East, with a chequered flag marking an unexploded bomb.

DIGGING FOR VICTORY: allotments in the shadow of the Royal Crescent symbolise the 'all-pull-together' spirit that saw Britain through the Second World War.

THE THEATRE ROYAL, Bath, reopened in 1982 after an extensive refurbishment which gave it the latest in stage technology, as well as restoring the auditorium to all its old glory. Much of the fund-raising was inspired by Mr Jeremy Fry, a Bath businessman, and Princess Margaret was guest of honour at a gala reopening night. Also in the picture with her and Mr Fry are the playwright Tom Stoppard and Dr Miriam Stoppard.

THE QUEEN'S SILVER JUBILEE of 1977 was celebrated at least as heartily as Victoria's anniversaries, and Bath had the bonus of a royal visit at the height of the summer. The smiles during a fancy dress contest at the Parade Gardens sum up the happy informality of the occasion.

ACKNOWLEDGEMENTS

Thanks for the loan of pictures, background information or other help are due to:

Avon County Council • Bath Reference Library • Heidi Best • Bristol United Press
Bruce Crofts • *Gloucestershire and Avon Life* • Norma Johnston • Peter Jones
Somerset and Avon Life • Michael J. Tozer • Mr C. Wheeler